The Fiddler's Trance

The Bucknell Series in Contemporary Poetry

This is one of a limited number of books of poetry of the highest quality published annually by the Bucknell University Press, in conjunction with *West Branch Literary Journal* and the Stadler Center for Poetry.

Titles in This Series

Karl Patten, *Touch*
Afaa Weaver, *The Ten Lights of God*
Charles Borkhuis, *Alpha Ruins*
Harryette Mullen, *Tree Tall Woman*
Katherine Soniat, *Alluvial*
Floyd Skloot, *The Fiddler's Trance*
Marc Hudson, *The Disappearing Poet Blues*

http://www.departments.bucknell.edu/univ_press

The Fiddler's Trance

Floyd Skloot

Lewisburg
Bucknell University Press
London: Associated University Presses

Associated University Presses
440 Forsgate Drive
Cranbury, NJ 08512

Associated University Presses
16 Barter Street
London WC1A 2AH, England

Associated University Presses
P.O. Box 338, Port Credit
Mississauga, Ontario
Canada L5G 4L8

The paper used in this publication meets the requirements of the American National Standard for Permanence of Paper for Printed Library Materials Z39.48-1984.

Library of Congress Cataloging-in-Publication Data

Skloot, Floyd.
The fiddler's trance / Floyd Skloot.
p. cm.—(Bucknell series in contemporary poetry)
ISBN 0-8387-5502-X (alk. paper)
I. Series.
PS3569.K577 F5 2001
811′.54—dc21 2001025306

PRINTED IN THE UNITED STATES OF AMERICA

For Beverly

What we call the beginning is often the end
And to make an end is to make a beginning.
The end is where we start from.
——T. S. Eliot, "Little Gidding"

Contents

III. Dancing in the Cosmos

Acknowledgments

My thanks to the editors of the following publications in which these poems first appeared:

America, The American Scholar, Atlanta Review, Blue Mesa Review, Chelsea, English Journal, Envoi (England), European Judaism (England), Flaming Arrows (Ireland), The Gettysburg Review, The Honest Ulsterman (Northern Ireland), The Hudson Review, The Iowa Review, JAMA: The Journal of the American Medical Association, The Journal, The New Criterion, New England Review, New Welsh Review (Wales), North American Review, Northwest Review, Poetry, Poetry Daily (on-line), Poetry Ireland Review (Ireland), Poetry Northwest, Poetry Nottingham (England), Poetry Wales (Wales), Portland Magazine, Portland Review, Prairie Schooner, Quarterly West, Rattle, The Sewanee Review, The Southern Review, Southern Poetry Review, Stinging Fly (Ireland), Tracks (Ireland), Verse, Virginia Quarterly Review and *Westerly (Australia)*.

"Mendelssohn at 38" appeared in *The American Scholar*.
"Dancing in the Cosmos" and "Poppies" appeared in *The Gettysburg Review*.
"Seed" and "The Yoga Exercise" appeared in *The Hudson Review*.
"Behind Gershwin's Eyes" and "The Fiddler's Trance" appeared in *The Iowa Review*.
"Currents" appeared in *The New Criterion*.
"Object Assembly" appeared in *The New England Review*.
"Self-Portrait in Opera Hat" appeared in *The North American Review*.
"Rasputin in Darkness" and "Remission" appeared in *Poetry*.
"Frost," "Juan Gris at 40, 1927," "Ravel at Swim" and "Since the Accident" appeared in *Poetry Northwest*.
"Gift" appeared in *The Sewanee Review* under the title "In Remission."
"Freud in London, 1939" and "Wild Blackberries" appeared in *The Southern Review*.
"December Dawn," "Delius and Fenby" and "The Tsar at Dawn" appeared in *The Virginia Quarterly Review*.

"The Tsar at Dawn" received the Emily Clark Balch Prize for Poetry from *Virginia Quarterly Review,* 2000.

Some of these poems appeared in the chapbooks *Bittersweet Nightshade* and *Poppies*. I am grateful to their editors, Larry Richman and Rodger Moody.

Centrum Foundation (Port Townsend, WA), Villa Montalvo (Saratoga, CA) and the Heinrich Böll Foundation (Achill Island, Ireland) provided artist residencies during the time these poems were written. I am also grateful to the Oregon Arts Commission for a 1993 Individual Artist Fellowship and to Oregon Literary Arts, Inc., for the 1996 William Stafford Fellowship in Poetry.

The Fiddler's Trance

I

Rasputin in Darkness

"In sickness, mind and body make a marriage."
—Robert Lowell, "In Sickness"

Rasputin in Darkness

After the Naproxen and Neurontin,
after the Ketoprofin,
the magnesium straight into my veins,
after Minor Blue Dragon
and flax seed oil
chased by low-fat cottage cheese,
after seven rounds
of acupuncture and a bed cushioned
by thick Swedish foam,
a mattress built of magnets,

after a spell in the place
where tides begin, just beyond the embrace
of light, a balance
point where the earth does not spin,

it was the middle
of the night and I was home,
staring out the window at moonlit oaks,
when I saw his beard ruffle
in a swirl of wind.

He wore a black cloth coat corded by rope
with a hint of crimson silk
at the throat. A great
golden crucifix sprouted from his breast
pocket with its chain
looped across the transverse piece.
He stood on the grass with fingers tangled
in his hair, nibbling
a sprig of parsley from our herb garden
and staring into the room.
A ring of icons dangled and glimmered
in the limbs above his head.

I heard the darkness fill with chanted prayers.
        It was possible to see
                him sway as his arms
rose like wings against the faint scaffolding
        of second growth behind him
and his fingers twitched when they reached for God.
                His eyes became stars.
Then they grew softer than air
                in the still moment
before storm and I knew he wanted to
        lay his healing hands on me.

He said *You have sent for me*
                and his voice was mist
on the glass that faded as he waited
        for me to open the door.
                All he wanted in return
was madeira and a few little sweets,
        potatoes boiled in their skins,
a platter of fish and fat samovar
        bubbling on the credenza.
                He wanted gypsy
music, wild dancing, a woman's laughter
                breathed into his ear.
He wanted my shaky tenor lifted
                in old Jewish songs
        that mourned a life I had lost.
Then he wanted the summer night to be
                long and luminous
        with soft Siberian light.

        My silence rose like a psalm
                on the delicate
tracery of my wife's breath in the bed.
                I turned back to her.
Rasputin whispered something to the trees
                and then it was dawn,
        the hoarse stanzas of western
tanagers mingling to a song of praise
        as sunlight suffused
the circle of shadow where he had stood.

Imperial Dreams

She loathed the tick of her parents' tall clock.
She loathed the sound of bubbling samovars.
Those closed rooms dense with the scent of black tea,
cut lemons, candles in sconces like stars
flickering at the edge of sight, her three
sisters clicking needles from dawn till dusk—

some days she could barely stand to be there
among them. To breathe their air. The jaded
glint in their half-shut eyes, frayed and faded
antimacassars cloaking every chair,
her shawled father mumbling his Sabbath prayer
while outside sleighs rushed through the falling snow
like women whispering to their Grand Dukes
and everyone else had someplace to go.

She imagined the Winter Palace loud
with manly laughter, silenced the instant
she appeared swathed in mauve silk. As the crowd
parted for her, she touched the abundant
hair in its tiara of fresh lilacs
and smiled at the Tsar. Women turned their backs,
but the Empress hailed her as a sister
and a lady-in-waiting admired her
diamond brooch. They asked her to sing the love
duet from the great *Boris Godunov*
arm-in-arm with a dark-whiskered Hussar.
She drank champagne with a Count from Pskov.
She flirted with the French Ambassador
and waltzed with a handsome young minister.

It was her mother humming in the hall
and her brother struggling over a phrase
on the battered piano. It was all
the fetid odors seeping through her days

and nights, the way they lingered on her skin,
mingled in every reverie, a thin
layer tainting all longing, all desire.

Her neverending summer nights became
nothing but neverending summer nights
and the glorious northern winter lights
only kept her from sleep. Pure tragedy
that she was cheated of life, that she
was left with nothing to protect her from
the cold except her raging inner fire.

The Secret Life

The women were always dancers
for the Bolshoi. Lean and lithe,
with enormous eyes, flaring tempers
and diamond tiaras in the evening hours,
such women were hard everywhere
their lovers were soft. There was
no cooking, no cleaning.
There were not even afternoons.

The men were always vast
with power, shielded by wealth
and moustaches, given to beef,
to raw spirits. Such men snored
even when they were awake.
There was always snow, wind
whistling through trees, and fog
on every window in the room.

Once in a while shots rang out.
Once in a while the wife showed up,
sobbing against a lintel or great
with rage in the dark backstage.
Once in a while there was a brother
to worry about, consumptive, fierce-eyed,
needing rest on a mountaintop.

Things never ended well. Trains shrouded
in steam, a crisis on the front, sudden
blood. Nothing but the sound of breath
coming and going in the stillness,
the darkness of a new moon, one last
flickering glance at the slowly ebbing tide
as music rose and the plush curtains closed.

Hunting Season

My neighbor's frenzied springer spaniels leap
and drop in turn like twins on a seesaw
when they sense me walking through the hip-deep
weeds between us. The autumn wind is raw
enough to bring tears. Walking the same crease
of hill at dawn a year ago I sensed
nothing wrong till I saw a stranger, face
blackened by grease, rifle cradled against
his chest, casing me as I stopped to catch
my breath. We are supposed to have a sense
of danger woven into our crosshatched
layers of axon and dendrite, a dense
net of mistrust as we move through the world.
In the chill air I watched his breath unfurl.

Sage

"Why should a man die who has sage in his garden?"
—14th Century Proverb

He loves to see the purple whorls of sage
in bloom, its knee-high woolly branches white
at noon, their stalked green leaves seeming to age
toward gray in the relentless summer light.

From his bed with its garden view he thinks
of bees that feed on sage to make a prized
honey, of sage juice for joint pain. He drinks
sage tea to prevent night sweats and to ease

his trembling, uses a wash of sage to soothe
sore gums and blacken graying hair. Nothing
helps, but he feels there is nothing to lose.
Burnt sage for the room, sage on scabs, smoking

sage cigarettes for his lungs, sage with roast
duck to cut the fat. He does not want to
live forever. What he wants is almost
more than he can say. A year, maybe two.

Object Assembly

"When we gaze at the world, we do not fathom the many layers of apparatus that underlie our unified visual experience, until neurological disease dissects them for us."

—Steven Pinker, *How the Mind Works*

They were five fingers and naked
fist palm down. They were wooden
bones too long in the grave, middle
and index still joined, the rest
adrift. They were a puzzle simple
as stark truth. He scattered them
before me, an offering from my own
future I could not assemble in time.

Nor could I assemble the Africa
that was a face without sense
organs, perhaps ears and nose
islands to the southeast, eye
afloat near Cape Verde. Time
was up before I found Madagascar.

Then I remembered summer dusks
spent shifting shades of blue
and red, hours finding patterns
centered around faded lilac
that became fields of fleur-de-lis
as jigsaw shape fitted to shape
and the familiar picture grew whole.
Monet came together in half
the time the box allowed.
My son, now the age I was then,
slapped hands across the card
table. Those days time was never
tight and my brain was intact.

Half a life later time reminds me
the temporal lobe scarred by virus
no longer functions as it should.
Rooms have walls in surprising
places and I get lost where I know
the way. These are called deficits.
Tests that would be games some other
time focus on what I cannot do.

So a Doctor of Psychology packs
the disassembled objects away beside
his blindfold and blocks I failed
to place in slots on a formboard
fast enough. He turns back to me,
knees to knees, flipping pictures
that have something missing I am
to name. I think the door should
have a wall around it but learn
later it should have had a knob.

Perhaps it is his face void
of expression, or his cracked
black bag of toys, or my young son
floating again near me with one
cerulean corner of sky cupped
in his palm. Perhaps I am tired.
But these tests at last reduce me
to tears like a child schneidered
by his father at gin rummy.

Self-Portrait in Opera Hat

"A man told me today that I never need write another note; I could make a fortune with my palette and brush."

—George Gershwin

Gershwin stands before his easel chewing
a fat cigar. Smoke, oil and turpentine
have thickened the air but he is doing
what he loves now. He remembers the fine
light on Folly Island, hearing it as
he hears music down through his long fingers
and sees himself come to life before his
own eyes. The paint is like the great singers
he has written for—it becomes pure song—
and this gray light is all he cares about
because it is perfect for the oblong
face staring back below the opera hat
and for the cluttered room, the tails, the hand
that paints the hand painting the mirrored hand.

Delius in Florida

Heavy heat and night haze off the St. John's
brought song to Solano Grove. Hunting quail
and alligator, Delius heard a panther's
rasp for the first time. At noon, a man
was whistling in thirds through the thatch
of a sagging cottage as Delius drove
his wagon past. There was a lyric wind
at dusk coming from the twisted oak
where the road home forked and deckhands
from passing steamships sang the Lord's praise.

All this black sound, and starless air,
and his father at last far across the dark
Atlantic. Perhaps music would be possible here,
its spirit awakening in him like a tropical dawn,
with sudden bursts of color. Or it might be
the magnolia scent, the twin palms shading
his verandah, even the withering orange
and pomelo crop only horses harvested.

How his father's wool-dusted jowls would
quiver in rage at the waste. He would buy
the whole estate! Head back, Delius imagined
his music-loving father, friend of Joachim,
still scheming to keep him in the family trade.
Learn to manage, he had whispered at bedtime
to his growing son. His father's hushed voice
was soon lost to the drone of cicadas deep
in the darkness and Delius the citrus farmer
closed his eyes, soaking up the close harmony
that rose from the river in place of the moon.

Odilon Redon in Charcoal, 1893

All night the sea is onyx streaked with teal.
Wind swirls sable. I hear cliffs turn jade.
I never want to wake again and feel
desire for light. I am forever afraid
light will overwhelm everything I see
the way the sharp odor of father's grapes
drenched my childhood in Bordeaux. I am free

of color now. Nothing vital escapes
my inward eye. Today charcoal trembles
in this hand, vibrates with all that is not
visible. It knows the way a daisy resembles
nothing so much as the smile of God.
It knows in the dark landscape of dreams
the world is precisely the way it seems.

Vigil

My brother's spirit floats
on the surface of his body
like the blade of a water lily.
I watch it ripple along his ribs
with each breath, waxy edge
lifting as if to break free.
There is nothing between life
and death now but a membrane
of faith like a lake's shifting
skin as night settles in,
wind folds down, and the first
hoots of owls are heard.

Wild Blackberries

In memory of my brother

In mid-July the blackberries were tart
and firm within their sweet surrounding flesh.
The full day's sun had just begun to mark
itself on the hidden red as a wish
for time, one week more at most, and warm nights
without rain. Thorns, leaves simple and lobed, dew
poised on dark branch tips framing the last white
flowers—everything reminded me of you
at the end, in a thicket of tubes, blood
spun clean for one more day, glistening hair
suddenly gray in a fan round your head.

The solstice brought a drenching rain as light
left summer behind. Berries draped with mold
shriveled to their stems and vines seemed to fold
in on themselves like dreams under the weight
of swarming yellowjackets. Here and there,
especially if my eyes were closed, I caught
a whiff of missing sweetness in the air.

Remission

When all my symptoms melt away like ice
that stilled our pond down to its hidden spring,
I find myself, as though a stranger twice
removed from life, believing everything

I see will remain as clear as it seems
in the shock of morning light. I am out
of season, feeling Spring when Fall sun gleams
off frost or an oak leaf with its stem caught

in a strand of spider web writhes before
the pumphouse door in swirling wind. The dark
edge of hope lurks where time springs shut. No more
incandescent visions, only the stark

truth of spring in my legs down a steep trail
and the clear sign of breath when I exhale.

Celestial North

Nights like this you could tell me time
is porous as gauze and I would believe
you. Tell me tonight has always happened
and always will be happening, since nothing
I know any longer says No. Whisper it
and I would believe you. Tonight the breeze
cooling us comes from the place where dreams
are harbored. Say this moment when winter
swivels into spring is genesis writ small,
say light is the center of darkness,
and I would turn toward it like a flower,
following your hand across the heavens
as it finds the north celestial pole.

The Yoga Exercise

Within a rushing stream of morning light
she stands still as a heron with one sole
held flush against the other inner thigh
and her long arms like bony wings folded
back so that when the motion of a breeze
passes through her body there is a deep

repose at its root and in an eye's blink
she has become this gently swaying tree
stirring in the wind of its breath while linked
to ground by the slow flow of energy
that brings her limbs together now in prayer
and blessing for the peace she is finding there.

Poppies

For years after a blaze, tree poppies
will spread brilliant yellow flowers
like the echo of flames in chaparral.
Camouflaged among crumbling bones of earth,
the pale salmon petals of pygmy poppies
thrive in thin alpine air. I have seen
acres of Oregon rainbows given over
to blind buds in hot southern sunlight,
cream cups tip their teeming bowls under
a sundown wind and prickly poppies turn
back cattle grazing a north Texas pasture.
I have been where winter rains stitch
a patchwork of Amapola del Campo
on the spring countryside. So I love
the moment your eyes close, when you become
the fire poppy whose buds must droop
before its flushed flowers will open.

Seed

She is alive. Although her doctors said
there was nothing to be done, she is home,
planting her summer garden, is not dead,
and plans to eat everything she has grown
in this plot, each carrot and tomato,
each squash, pepper, lettuce leaf. She will live
beyond the harvest and what will not grow
is her tumor, its flowers held captive
and still beneath her heart. Only the live
wire of her will separates her now from
the future displayed in black and white five
months ago, backlit clearly. It will come
sooner or later, but this is her time
to cultivate and seed. She is alive.

The Fiddler's Trance

—after Chagall

The air above Vitebsk was filled with Jews
gassed green. From the synagogues and orchards,
rubble of butcher shops, from crushed forges,
charred barns and wooden huts rose the blues
and blazing yellows of the world to come.
Red footprints racing nowhere across snow
were chased by spirals of dark fire that no
one saw in time. Every bird was struck dumb
by dawn. Chagall remembered the future
before ever leaving home. Yet he knew
song was possible. Whatever was true
about the sound of night, he would picture
one lonely fiddler looming and entranced
to find himself the center of a dance.

The Tsar at Dawn

The sound that wakes me is a doe leading
    her two fawns through the mantle
of oak and maple leaves shrouding my yard.
        I turn to see her
freeze, then flee through a crease of dripping fir
    with her young leaping after—

and into a shaft of brilliant sunlight
    walks Nicholas, head down, hands
clasped behind his back, hunting for mushrooms.
    He stops to stretch his shoulders
        and neck as though just
    awake from the deepest sleep.
        The man loves nothing
so much as such mornings after hard rain,
    dew glistening on the grass,
        undulating lines
    of honking Canada geese
        passing overhead,
and the rash salute of mushrooms at dawn.

    He does not know where he is,
or where his guard of Don Cossacks has gone,
        or why the weather
is so mild for this time of year, no snow
        so far into fall,
    or even that I lie here
        while my fever spikes
watching him bend to inspect a circle
    of creamy white fairy rings.

    He has been haunting the woods
all week. The blue of his eyes is a dream
        of clear winter skies

softening to the shade of solstice prayers
        as the day drags on,
    then lakewater in mountain
craters or the flowers of Russian sage
    where he has stopped now to kneel.
        Those shut umbrellas
are shaggy manes, best if gathered when young.

You can see he is a man who welcomes
    time alone. Last night, when trees
        swaying in the wind
set off the motion sensors, I wondered
        at first if it was
his wandering that filled the night with light,
    if it was his voice I heard
keening somewhere in the middle distance
    for his wife and five children
lost forever in a summery flash.

He rises again, a ragged darkness
    at the knees of his trousers,
and finds himself drawn to a bright cluster
    of puffballs where the land dips
down to our abandoned apiary.
    From behind, he looks younger
than I am, straight-backed and thick in the trunk,
    a man with time on his hands.
I remember moving like that nine years
ago, before the first signs of illness.

        Perhaps he has come
    to take me away with him,
        returning me to
a place beyond the Pale of Settlement.
        Perhaps he has come
    to teach me that I must love
        him, though he never
    meant my people anything
but harm. He may have come for nothing more
    than to linger in these woods

that have been helping
me heal. The kid leather of the puffball's
mass draws him down, makes him smile
as he reaches out to stroke its smooth white
flesh in search of the tell-tale
cracks and yellow tinge
that would be the first signs of bitterness.

II

The True World

"A sickbed is a grave, and all that the patient says there is but a varying of his own epitaph."

—John Donne, *Devotions Upon Emergent Occasions*

Behind Gershwin's Eyes

"Nobody else smelled burning garbage because Gershwin's olfactory sensation came from a slow-growing tumor on the right temporal lobe of his brain."

—Joan Peyser, *The Memory of All That*

They did not believe him.
They told him the smell
of burning garbage was all
in his head. Some mornings
it was all he could do
to lift his head from
the pillow. Some nights
his brain was on fire,
songs he thought would take
a hundred years to write
suddenly aflame behind
his bulging eyes.

Dizzy in the barber's
chair, dizzy before
the chorus, dizzy
on the tennis court.

They did not believe him
even when he was adrift
in the first movement
of his Concerto in F.
He felt darkness beyond
the footlights seep
into his soul, nothing
but a sea of dream
everywhere, and heard
the echo of unplucked
strings, a quiver

of timpani dying out
quickly as one long
note from an oboe
wafted heavenward.
Then he found himself
back in Los Angeles,
familiar body still
upright on the piano stool,
Smallens with his baton
frozen at the shoulder,
only to blunder again
in the andante and they
told him nothing was wrong.

Dizzy in the Brown
Derby, dizzy before
the surf, dizzy
in the swimming pool.

They believed he was
not happy in Hollywood.
There is nothing wrong
with Gershwin that a song
hit wouldn't cure.
It was in his head, he was
lovelorn or he was riddled
with guilt, he was balding
and drooling, muddle-headed
by noon, listless underneath
the stars. They believed
him sapped by motion picture
making and longing for New
York City. Those hands
once a blur on the keyboard
could only move slow as flowers
toward the sun yet nothing
was wrong. In the spring
those sandaled feet
that could only shuffle
in the summer garden

had been quick as flame
to his own new music
yet nothing was wrong.

A blade of light
where the drawn shades
meet. Roses without odor,
icewater leaping from its cut
glass goblet, eyes leached
of luster in the shadowy
mirror of his brother's eyes.
He spread chocolates melted
in the oven of his palm
up his arms like an ointment,
and soon he was gone.

Ravel at Swim

"The inability to communicate speech, writing or music when the peripheral nervous system is largely undamaged is called an aphasia."
—"Maurice Ravel: Aspects of Musical Perception," by John O'Shea

Something dark has stolen the sea from me.
Always a seal in water, I found its
melodies and swam open harmony
through them. Now I flail. Nothing I do fits

the rhythms around me. *Swiss Watchmaker,*
they called me for the design of my work.
Mere lover of wind-up toys, a baker
of sweets, as though elegance were a quirk.

Now the hand that holds forks by their tines floats
like driftwood on the sea of music spread
before me. It will not write down the notes
I hear like a gulls' bent tones in my head.

It will not play what I see on paper
and know I wrote two years ago to be
performed one-handed. (That was a caper!
I loved having such limits placed on me.)

It will not sign my name. It tries to light
a match with the tip of a cigarette.
What is left? It took me eight days to write
a fifty-six word letter I have yet

to end, consoling a friend whose mother
just died. I do not want to be seen now
by anyone who knew me at another
time. Pure artifice, they said, missing how

my need for form affirmed the passions of
my heart. They must not see me with the link
from brain to limb severed and all I love
lost. Sheer formlessness surrounds me. I think

but cannot share my thoughts. I remember
every flower's fragrance, the taste of lamb
roasted for hours over charcoal embers
at summer bazaars, lips on mine, but am

powerless to express myself. Let me
be alone. Let me have the grace of pure
music in my head, where I hear and see
perfectly. That silence I can endure.

Starry Night

"Perhaps I might really recover if I were in the country for a time."
—Vincent Van Gogh

Tonight the moon throbs with light
it seizes from stars as they rise
and the cypresses grow holy
before my eyes. Wind fills the sky.
I see clouds shudder, houses
and shops cower, but somehow
high grass finds its own source
of stillness. I think it is violet
in nature. Never has there
been such a night for seeing
how the dark world thrives
when day's brilliance dies
and sight fully becomes surprise.

Who would want all these deep blues
to soften as though toward dawn?
No dawn will bring along
a day as pure again. Who would
want to be well enough to lose
such hues? I know a man can
be so far from madness the true
world cannot find him. I know
he will be saved only when
the moon collects enough radiance
to render heaven tangible
as the breath of sunflowers.

Look: there is a glow inside
the emptiest spaces when we
study their darknesses. There is
also a hush no stroke of

a painter's brush can muffle.
Think of the instant swallows
rising above a field you enter
suddenly loop back in unison—
a thick landscape of faith
that is beyond words, yet explains
why I am standing here at all.

The Tangerines

Not the dead-pan gaze
of the blonde barmaid
nor the black ribbon
loose around her neck,
not the thick-set man
in the gilded mirror
who holds her gaze
nor the vase of cut
pink and white roses,
dark stoppered bottles
of Bass ale and champagne,
not the creme de menthe,
not even the slippered
legs of the trapeze artist
dangling above blurry
patrons in their evening
gowns and tailcoats,

but the tangerines
filling a crystal compote
on the marble-topped bar
of the Folies-Bergère
in the last large work
by Edouard Manet, stilled
as he was with syphilis,
hands losing all power
to hold a paintbrush,
legs lanced by pains,
eyes finding a sign of life
that grief would not distort.

Freud in London, 1939

There is pain in his mouth and jaw,
intimate pain beyond reach of drugs.
He has known it would kill him
since the first signs that distant summer
his grandson died. Torment in the snout
and heart these sixteen years and nothing
but work to compensate. There is Anna
still unmarried. Adler, Abraham, Ferenczi,
all of them dead and Jung running wild
in the Alps. At night, sirens in the air.
All day, soft voices of farewell in the air.

He thought it would be easier to die.
But there are sons still at large in Germany,
Moses to be explained, and belief in God,
and evil on a scale even he could imagine
in theory only. There is the lure of sleep
and dreams. There is hunger for silence.

He is free but knows he will never recover
from leaving his beloved Vienna behind.
Never recover from the agony in his bones
or the smell that seeps from his wounds.
The dog will no longer come near.
Who can blame him? The flesh melts
as though practicing for death and light
here is never good. The world's borders
are all gone, the Great War settled like ash
on the crotch of history, and the mind
twists around its most secret desire.
Schur with his morphine hovers in the dark.

Delius & Fenby

"To be a genius, as this man plainly was, and have something beautiful in you and not be able to rid yourself of it because you could no longer see your score paper and no longer hold your pen—well, the thought was unbearable!"

— Eric Fenby, *Delius As I Knew Him*

Always toward sunset Delius grew
restless and uneasy in his carriage
chair, raving at the pain in his legs,
flicking his long tapering fingers
as though stating a theme on the air.
His proud head, pale as marble,
began to wobble no matter the effort
to hold it still. He demanded a thick
rug for warmth. He demanded a thin rug
for comfort, then demanded that no
rug touch him, all the time wanting
me to read one more story aloud
like a child refusing to go to bed.

Delius required that everything
be just so. His bean and barley
soup must be salted in the pot
and served piping hot. No rattling
cups or clattering spoons at table,
where chitchat lashed him to fury.
After dinner, one cigar and a slow
push up the Marlotte road in silence,
when even the neighbor's great Alsatians
walked hushed beside us. Saturdays
we could play only Sir Thomas Beecham's
records of Delius on the gramophone
in the quiet of his music room.

One morning in the faded garden
where Delius sat beneath the elder
tree, I could see that he was angry
with me. Tossing his head from side
to side, he champed and glared
toward the rising sun, clearing
his throat *fortissimo*. At night
a melody had come on the verge
of sleep, making him weep to be
hearing new music leap in his mind
again. But I overslept beneath
the full-sized face of mad Strindberg
by Munch, dreaming myself south
to Paris amidst a wild summer storm,
surrounded by young friends in good
health, rain playing a sudden cadenza
on the swollen Somme and the thunder
in E-Flat. I wanted tea.

My hair still damp, my face creased
by sleep, I took up paper and pen
without a word. I sat cross-legged
on the grass wondering whether Delius
would sing to me. Would he call out
the notes and their time-values?
At last I was to do what I had come
from Scarborough to do and free him
of the music. He threw his head
back like a wild horse in flight
and neighed toneless to the sky.
"Hold it!" he said, causing me
to drop my pen, then he bayed
toward heaven again. I heard
neither words nor notes, only
a shapeless cry. He could not
bring forth the tune he heard!
Dazed, all I could say was
"Delius, what key is it in?"
"A minor, Fenby, don't be slow."

Fingers inky, spectacles blurred
by tears, I confess being blind
as Delius himself when I groped
for the sanctuary of his porch.
Of course, in time we learned
to bring forth his music, imagining
ourselves on cliffs in the heather
looking out over the sea, knowing
chords in the high strings were
a clear sky. But I shall never
forget Delius, a shrunken relic,
mouth opened in anguish, gripped
by the awful beauty inside him.

Juan Gris at Forty, 1927

In the softening geometry
of heart valves lay the secret
to his late genius. Loss is all
arranged on the earthly plane,
its colors serene in a light
that is always about to fade.
Behind him now are years
crisp from edge to edge.
Behind him are zinc bars
and demitasse to the lip
of a cracked white cup,
dominoes, the precise risk
inherent in collage. Home
for good, each breath
like the stroke of a brush,
each motion measured
against the whole shape
of day. Before him now
are days coming too soon
to an end. Before him
he finds by chance shards
in a trapezoid of bedroom
mirror, finds apples cozy
as lovers in a tub, his pipe
perfectly balanced on its shank,
a book's pages fanning
open of their own weight
on a table tilted into the dark.

Mendelssohn at 38

"On 1 November 1847, Mendelssohn's condition rapidly deteriorated. He experienced the first of a series of strokes."

—John O'Shea, "The Mendelssohn Family"

I look back on the promise of my youth
(*Felix* the fortunate) and am so tired.
A boy in auburn ringlets playing fugues
for old Goethe, a boy with liquid fire
in his hands! I glimpsed myself in glacier
wind and flood waters under the slender
Devil's Bridge. I loved the wild allegro,
the clack of trains, wind in a seaside cave.
Swiss sunlight, Monti Albani's sweet air,
Loch Lomond. I found music everywhere.
Now some mornings I am too weak to fold
back my bedsheets. There is nothing I crave
as much as silence. Not even pine trees,
the rich smell of old stones with moss upon
them, or the sight of snowy peaks would please
me. Quiet, like the moment before song
stretched out forever. Stillness, that instant
before strings quiver. This is what I want.

Weber in London, Spring 1826

"I am now a broken machine."
—Carl Maria Von Weber (1786–1826)

I want to be home before my breath gives
out. I want to see Lina and my son.
Dear God, I must breathe in the sweet Dresden
air, warm and dry in June. A man who lives
for music dies into the same silence
as one who lives for God or sword. My work
is done. There is nothing beyond the dark
to fear, nothing to lose. The opulence
of oblivion seems heaven to me
as my feet swell, my hands shake and I reek.
I am the color of wheat. Lifeblood leaks
from me everywhere and now I can see
sleep is no use. It is time for me to
begin the journey. I came here to earn
money for my family but I yearn
for one thing only. Bring me home to you.

III

Dancing in the Cosmos

I have come to a still, but not a deep center,
    A point outside the glittering current.
                    —Theodore Roethke, "The Far Field"

Punta Cahuita

Silt that blocks sunlight is killing
brain coral clinging to the outer
edges of reef at Punta Cahuita.
I follow a trail that wedges itself
inland past the Rio Suarez, cutting
through swamp forest that teems
with three-toed sloths, coatimundi
and howler monkeys. But all I hear
and see is the fresh memory of blue
parrot fish crushing a thick shelf
of moose horn coral using their fused
teeth like beaks. I might as well be
walking along East Chicago streets
for all I notice here on the edge
of the Caribbean Sea. Then the trail
meets a small stream and a Jesus Christ
lizard rises startled on its hind legs
to run across the water's surface.

It happens so fast that all I can do
is laugh. Its frilled crest is fluffed
above the bright green back like a sail
as it runs, a tiny dinosaur, and leaps
off the water to vanish in undergrowth.
I stop. There is movement everywhere,
sound everywhere. The world is back
and I am back in the world. High
in the trees a green ibis sings
a song of welcome like the gurgling
of cool water poured from bottles
the same shade as the bird heading
now toward the suddenly visible sky.

Currents

The great blue heron rides a cottonwood
limb downriver. She spins through a circle
of sunlight as her mate's wide loops dazzle
the morning and his hoarse squawk says he would
join her if he could. He swoops close to see
again there is no room. She turns her long
neck slower than the limb turns in the strong
current, keeping him in sight as though she
imagines currents of air mimic dark
river currents she will dare when the time
comes. He moves like a dancer past his prime,
a beat slow for her and just off the mark,
but game while she waits against the measure
for a moment they can enter together.

Frost

Wizened, spoiling for a fight, Frost is here
again. I have tried adjusting my pain
medication and sleep schedule, but still
he comes back to wander these woods like wind
stirring the Douglas fir. There is a gleam
of cold light where he stops and squats to track
the cries of naked oak that lean against
a surge of squalls.
                                        I hear him rhyming oak
with choke, then smoke and cloak as he looks down
into the valley. It will grow slowly
visible with the lifting of morning
mist and he will allow himself a small
smile. Spoke. Broke.
                                        Finally he turns to me,
lifting his chin to indicate the rough
grove at my back. "I see you lost your bees."
I nod as though I always speak with ghosts.
"They were gone before I got here."
                                                                        Frost first
showed up with late September's heavy rain,
a creature of the equinox, I thought,
till I got a closer look. He follows
his own timetable like the pack of deer
that comes and goes now hunting season has
ended.
            "You need some chickens," he whispers.
"Good layers kept me and mine alive through
lean years." He leads me straight uphill. Baroque.
Folk. Roanoke. "Awoke," I say and he
stops dead to let me know who makes the rules.

Then his face unfolds, thawing as he seems
to grow young before my eyes. "Like your cane,"

he says, and winks when he adds "don't tell me:
Hazel from Rapallo in honor of
Ezra Pound." He shakes his shaggy head. Yoke.
Hoax. "They let him go when I told them to."

Because I have been reading Freud I know
this is the key. First illness, then prison,
then being freed by Frost. Wish-fulfillment,
the heart of every dream. He makes his way
toward a pile of pine and points to the axe.
Stroke. Soak. "Running low." I turn to find him
drifting west with the sun and well beyond
reach of my voice. "There is more seasoning
behind the gazebo," I tell thin air
and watch another morning shape itself
around the twist of winter on the wind.

Bee Purple

"Bees' eyes can pick up much of what ours can,
but in addition they can see a wavelength of light,
a color, impossible for us to perceive."

—Philip J. Hilts, *Memory's Ghost*

Deep in a montane forest two bees flit
among the sego lilies, seeing dark
purple crosses where all we see are white
petals tinged sometimes with hints of lilac.
In early summer these showy flowers
are bells ringing where the mountain towers
above us and we are deaf to it all.

Perhaps this soil is singing. Perhaps June
ends with scents of lavender and heal-all
even though we cannot smell them, and soon
wind feels exactly like the sea. We call
this sundown. We welcome the full moon
fading to a white we have learned to doubt,

the flash of gray blue pinyon jays whose short
quavering laugh is what ushers us out
of the pines and into the world we thought
we knew. We welcome night. The vast silence
is filling with sound as our still world spins.

Christmas Choir

The smoky contralto sheds her leather
jacket and wraps a scarf around her throat
for warmth, complaining about the weather
while a soprano frets over the note
she could not reach last week. The twin brother
of the choir master hammers out a few
chords of *Limehouse Blues* to get his fingers
loose and refuses to talk to the young
female tenor, one of the best singers
they have found in years, who wrapped her long
legs around him last night but called him Jack
instead of Raymond. Meanwhile another
brother can be heard rehearsing a new
solo in the narthex, his baritone
spilling like December light down the nave.
They noticed he was again dressed in black,
mourning, rumor has it, a dead lover.
One bass and his tenor wife will be gone
opening night; both mezzo-sopranos believe
they will miss the same Thursday performance,
since it is the first night of Chanukah,
and the choir master himself is not sure
his wife can sing because there is a chance
the growth on her left tonsil will require
surgery. But here they are together
on the chancel, coughing and murmuring,
their voices warm now, coming together,
rising and falling, and they begin to sing.

Since the Accident

Anomia, the inability to name objects, is caused
by injury to the inferior frontal gyrus.

—*The Merck Manual*

Ah this, this is the thing you might pour
soup in to heat up, or water for tea.
First you have to light the flame on the box
where people cook. Those? They slip on your sox
and then you have to bend and tie them tight.
Well, with those on the lower part of your
arm, of course. Yes. A part of the body,
sure enough, you can also count with them.
Fingers? If you say so. That could be right.
I know what is happening. This notebook,
see, I draw pictures of things and then look
them up when I get stuck. It's a real shame,
but this is how I have been, day and night,
since the accident. I just lost the names
of everything. Except for butterflies,
which is what I do not understand. Why?
Nelson's Hairstreak, Swallowtail or the Bay
Checkerspot. No problem. Wood Nymph, Pine White,
the Northern Blue in a field of lupine,
California Sister—the names come out fine.
Show me a specimen; I can tell you
what it is without thinking. But to say
ankle? That is something I could not do
if you asked me to. I cannot do it.
A blank. I did? Maybe by accident,
or how I breathe. The way I still can cry.

December Dawn

I know this fog is here because last night
was clear and cold. It has nothing to do
with runaway virus, the swollen white
matter of my brain, or another new
year of illness—my fourth—leading nowhere
I wish to go. Walking the riverbank,
passing an old man who is always there
at dawn with his German shepherd and blank
stare, I know where I am. I also know
fog is water vapor spewed when moist air
cools to its dew point. I know the limbo
viruses populate is based somewhere
between the living and dead. A billion
billion viruses would fill one Ping-Pong
ball. I know. And also the vermilion
hull of a sailboat named *Wayfarer's Song*
is invisible now though I can hear
wind through its mast harmonize with a gull's
cry. It is not the paved walkway that veers
left but my body swayed by the brain's pull.
But still, I have never felt so strongly
before that the world has become nothing
but an image of what is inside me.
I'll walk until the fog lifts or something.

Consultation

The surgeon draws an S in ink across
my sole precisely where his incision
will be. As my toes curl, he says the mass
is flush against bone and enmeshed in nerves,
but firm. This pleases him. How long has
it been there, he wonders, probing again,
eyes closed. His hand moves with precision
down my instep, where tendons stretch, and curves
back over the arch. Like a magician,
he distracts me with his gestures and voice,
making nothing of something, moving fast,
all patter and smiles. He shifts position
and my foot is bathed in harsh light that flows
past his shoulder, accenting the high gloss
given off by my skin over the growth.

Lime at the Edges

Lime at the edges,
a world washed in citrus light
as though spring
burst
this year on the brink of time.

Something to do with looking
straight
at the source.
Something to do with breaching
the thin sheath
of air, a season given
over to
more heat than ever before.

I do not like being still
this morning
here where the river
bends west but I must
rest
a while in the gathering
wind.
Where is the belted
kingfisher
hovering over water
like a hummingbird?
Where is the tiger
swallowtail sipping nectar
from the blackberry
vine, or the silver salmon?

I need to see the pale gloss
of false dawn,
hues

well-known from a life
by the sea.
I need something familiar
seen
from the corner of my eye,
something the color of faith.

Lime at the edges
with not even a hint of blue.
I may have looked
too long last night
at the full
moon in all its glory.

In the Phoenix Islands

Canton's lagoon is thick with damselfish.
Hermit crabs scavenge beside frigate birds
and nesting fairy terns. Do we still wish
we were there, cooled by trade winds, and that words

did not matter? If lizards overrun
the ruined Air Force base, so what? If drought,
saline well water, and a blinding sun
conspired to drive a thousand British out,

isn't this still our dream place? Triggerfish,
a coral atoll, a place in the sun.
Suppose we were allowed to have this wish
come true. Forget the guano quarries. Run

away together to the Phoenix chain.
Love, suppose we lived alone with our pain.

Dawn at Sligo Bay

Here a sky boiling sapphire
from the sea is flecked apple
and carmine, surging where it
is shot through with bolts
of sun. The dark shore
and its claw of land stand
no chance against a dawn
drawn like this from earth's
royal core. This is a blue
so deep it mauls all light
and bursts white to the eye.

Now in the very last moment
Sligo Bay can hold daybreak
back, the cliff crumbles.
Its colors blend in a creamy
plunge the scored sea never
seems to notice. Near shore,
breakers thicken and gleam.

There is nothing smooth or still
about the way sunrise lures
mist and sheen from drenched
rocks or tames the tidal bulge.
This should be the dawn a man
sees when he believes himself
free of memory at last. Let it
wash over him like harsh ocean
wind and he will not turn away,
even when a woman whose face
glows golden in the growing light
waves a bonnet the same raven
black the night leaves behind.

The Landscape of Silence

There is a silence thin enough
to pierce the loudest cry. I heard
it first at night within the surf,
a secret of the sea, one word
whispered through breakers like the hiss
of foam. I heard it as the wish

moonlight makes in the folds of waves.
Once I heard it in the center
of a thunderstorm as roof eaves
gave. I felt a fury enter
the heart of my dream, but the still
place held. It was like a deep well

echoing the sound of my breath
long after I had walked away.
Silence called me back to myself,
revealing the edges as day
is revealed in the new moon's light.
And I heard it again tonight

in the winds of County Mayo
as scarlet flowers from the wild
fuchsia poured through my closed window
in a dream. I sat up to find
evening shadows in the middle
of the night. Time is a riddle

they spoke in my ear. Its answer
is shadows and flowers from dreams,
silence in bells of wild fuchsia
pealing around me till it seems
I have grown deaf to all other
sounds but the plainsong of wonder.

Beyond Grande Ronde

At the edge of town
a white horse wearing half
its winter coat shivers
in the sundown wind.
The field behind her,
stippled with shadow,
shows precisely where
autumn has lost its grip.

We drive west as high
clouds flush and blanch,
choked on the light
thickening before our eyes.
Fifty now, I have learned
it is the promise
of storm, not storm itself
that stills faith in the last
hour, the last breath.

We slow when the road
narrows, dips and rises
into a purer air.
The swollen river curves
away only to return just
as the road curves away.
Singing together, we climb
into the Coast Range
and a deeper darkness
just over the summit.

Cipole Road in Early Spring

Day by day sunlight reclaims the drowned
onion field, raising hilltop islands of oak,
softening caked folds of dyke that hold
Cipole Road in place. Like lost memory,
color seeps and blots at the water's edge.
Two months ago I saw a man steer his boat
in a direct line from here toward a swollen
sun pinned on the tip of Mount Hood
and bleeding alpenglow. It faded from view
as though drained in a blink of the eye
and the man merged with thickening shadows
at the far end of the field. As the road rises
toward a shimmer of streetlights on the far
side of the hill, I see the flicker of white wings
where a vee of geese banks and heads north.

Eola Valley at Dusk

First the sound, then the shadow,
then the cruciform shape
of the old cropduster passes
through a shaft of sun
in the valley below.
I watch it rise, flashing light,
leaving behind a faint mist
that settles in one long
last breath. To the west,
the first hint of red sky
becomes a blush that thickens
as the plane banks and turns
back for another pass.

The Downed Fir

It was the wind. It was the rain.
It was the icy winter night.
Out of the dark we heard a train
on tracks forged from the embers
    of childhood terror
bolt through our woods like flashing light.
    It was late December,
early January, the turn
of the year because we used our
new goose down comforter and burned
Christmas candles till the power
    came back. Now I remember.
We felt the house shudder and thought
    earthquake. Then we said
it was the storm. Never the echo
of two giant Douglas fir brought
down arm in arm. We did not know
    till this afternoon,
walking the vanished winter creek
backwards to its source, when we saw
the downed fir twisted in a heap
of tangled limb and trunk, earth raw
    where the roots mushroomed
skyward in a soiled howl of dread.
March sunlight swarmed through the still bare
canopy, drenching path, deadfall,
moss, dry creek bed, ferns, here and there
the first shoots of wild iris all
    over the hillside.
    At the same time
a frigid north wind curried the thin
leaves of evergreen like a comb.
Time seemed to crack and lay open
as we turned together toward home.

Dancing in the Cosmos

At first I thought the new
moon was pulling us straight
toward the cosmos in bloom
and singing at your yard's
edge. Then I heard the tune
rising. We began to swirl
in a warm whirlwind, sheer
scarves encircling us
like the visible scent
of snapdragons and sword
lilies all crimson, pink
and yellow where your hillside
buckles valleyward.

A sudden shift in tempo
let us spare the lacy
crowns of fennel bent
to our waists by the weight
of their seeds and left us
meshed in raspberry vines.
One look and again I knew
we would soon be hopelessly
deep in the feathers
and petals of the cosmos.

But I believed the music
filling the night was saying Give
in, spin through the cosmos
with faith we will not harm
even the palest wildflower
with our inspired capers.
I believed because the clear
sky we slept under this summer
was still teeming with wild

harmonies. Bats swooped
to owl shrieks and the Milky
Way soaked up the moon's
last offering of light.
So the land was going dry.
So the sun was hotter than ever.
Such nights, such alien dancing,
and never did we lose
a single frilled floret.

Gift

This is a spring he never thought to see.
Lean dusky Alaskan geese nibbling grass
seed in his field, early daffodils, three
fawns moving across his lawn in the last
of afternoon light, everything he had
let go with small ceremonies on dark
September nights has suddenly come back.
The taste on his tongue is of tamarind
chutney, fish curry, clove, tangs he adores
above all else. He smells the hyacinth
and can feel hope with the terrible crack
of a thawing river loosen in his heart.
He imagines sailing among the Queen
Charlottes come April, tacking into wind
that is the kindest he has ever known,
then gentle breakers, golden sanded shores.